Louis Moyse Flute Collection

Louis Moyse

THE FLUTIST'S PRIMER

Easy and Melodious Exercises

Based on Scales and Arpeggios (in all Keys) with optional 2nd Flute or Piano Accompaniment

ED-3077

ISBN 0-7935-5005-X

G. SCHIRMER, *Inc.*

DISTRIBUTED BY
HAL•LEONARD® CORPORATION
7777 W. BLUEMOUND RD. P.O. BOX 13819 MILWAUKEE, WI 53213

Foreword

DEBUSSY used to call scales and arpeggios "The Divine Arabesques . . .". They are the basic "tools" used by composers for centuries, and are the root of music written since the Renaissance.

It was soon realized that they formed THE system needed and thus established and condensed as necessary means for practice of instrumental technique.

It is advised that they be approached without fear, and not be rebuffed as "exercises," on the contrary, one should consider them not only as the best way to improve technique on any instrument, but as the means by which one can develop a better and deeper understanding of music.

These duets, based on simple chords, supporting a simple melodic and musical line, changing patterns and dealing with various articulations, will effortlessly lead the beginner flutist to a greater and rewarding achievement.

Beginners on any instrument like to play music written in simple keys of no more than one or two sharps or flats, but a great deal of music is composed in the other keys, and in order to be able to read all music, one has to learn how to deal with this difficulty.

In this book the order of scales including sharps and flats is progressive:

No. 1 is in C Major and A minor
No. 2 in G Major and E minor (1 sharp)
No. 3 in F Major and D minor (1 flat)
No. 4 in D Major and B minor (2 sharps), etc.

The student may enjoy playing these melodious exercises with someone other than his or her teacher; both 2nd flute and piano parts are easy to sight read.

We also want to emphasize that these exercises are *not* composed in trio form; they should be played as duets either with a 2nd flute accompaniment, or with piano accompaniment only.

LOUIS MOYSE

To Heather Allen-Moyse

The Flutist's Primer

Easy and Melodious Exercises based on Scales and Arpeggios (in all keys) with optional 2nd flute, or piano accompaniment

Louis Moyse

PART I

1
C Major - A minor

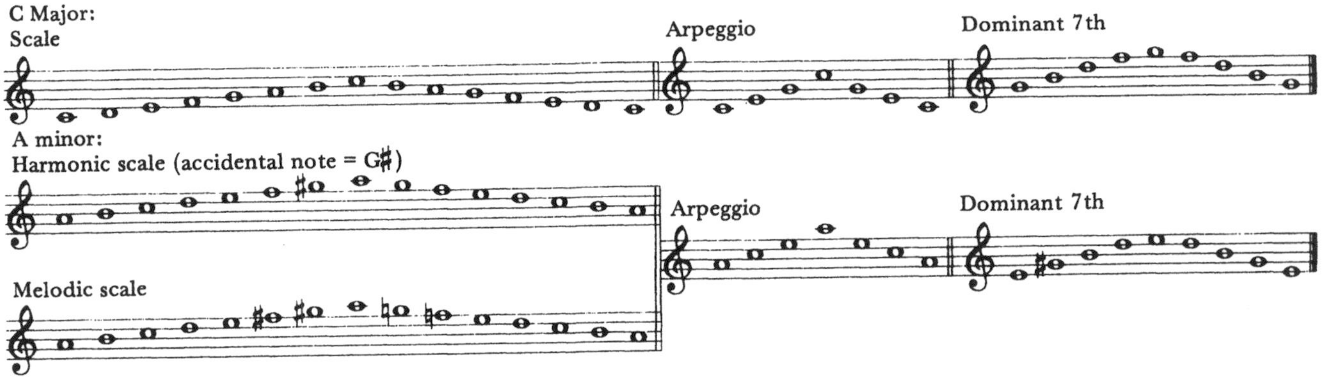

A minor

2
G Major - E minor
(1 sharp=F]

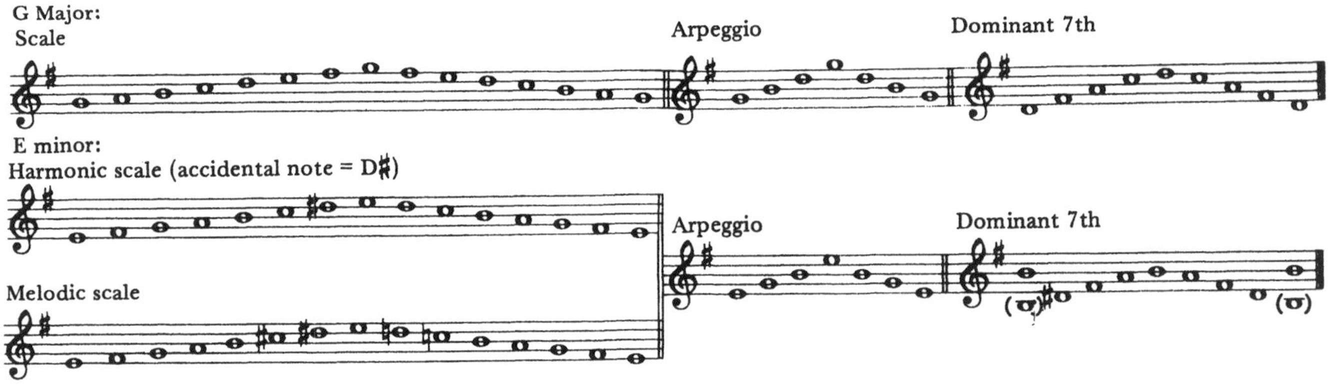

E minor

3
F Major - D minor
(1 flat = B)

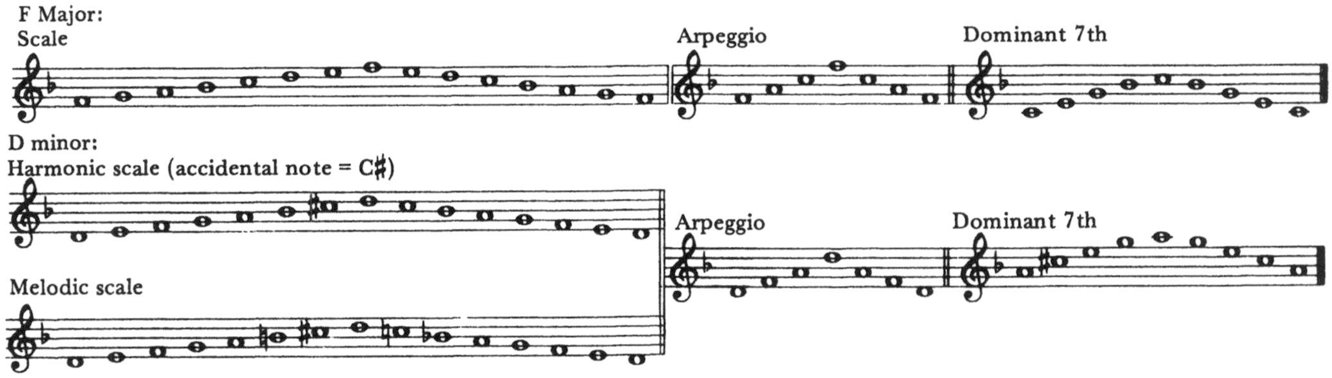

D minor

4
D Major - B minor
(2 sharps = F, C)

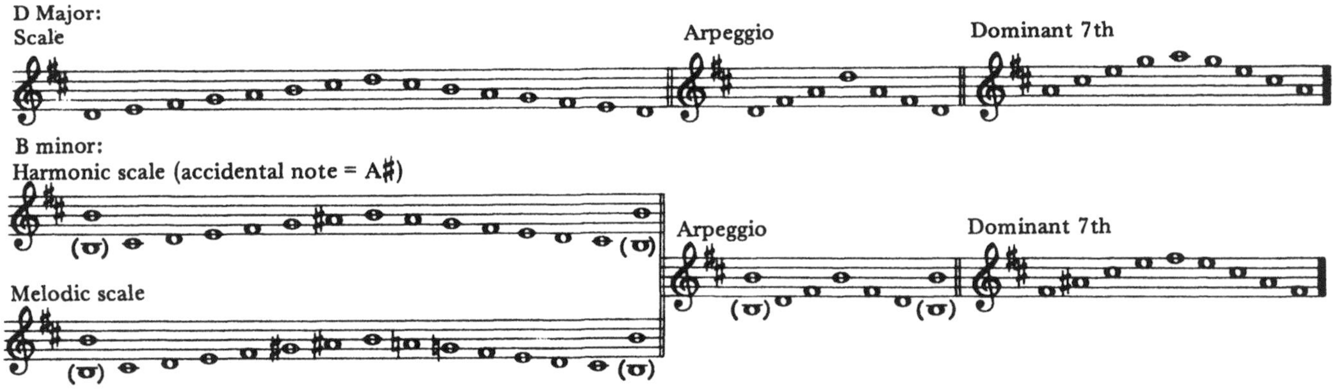

B minor

5
B♭ Major - G minor
(2 flats = B, E)

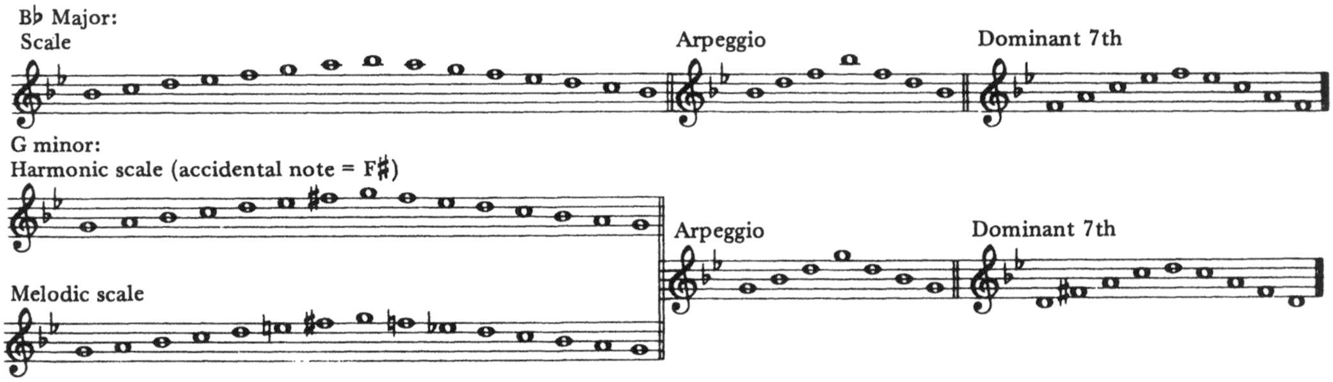

G minor

6
A Major - F# minor
(3 sharps = F, C, G)

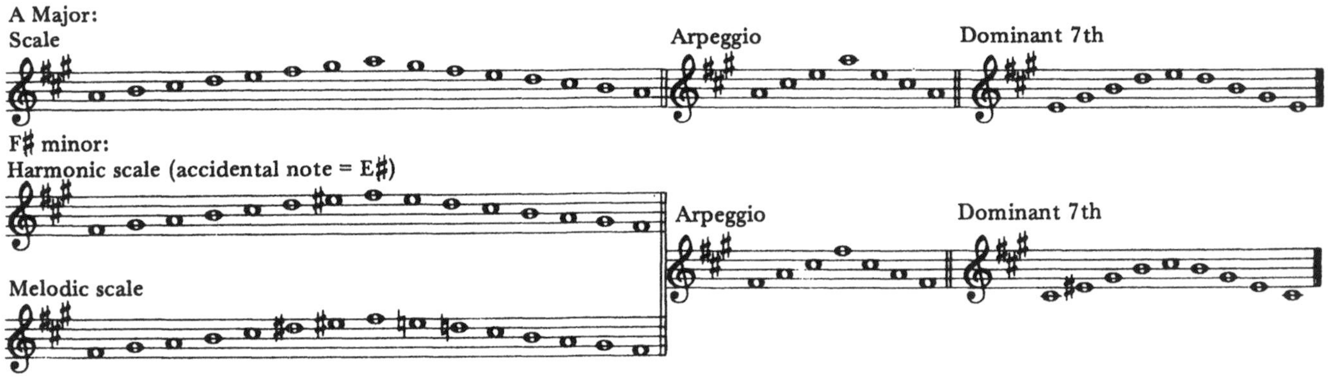

F# minor

7
E♭ Major - C minor
(3 flats = B, E, A)

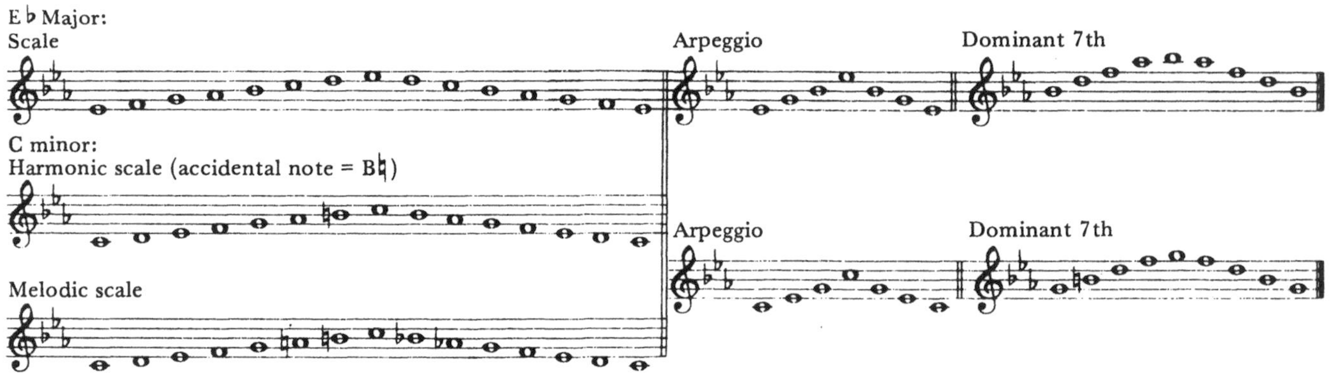

C minor

8
E Major - C♯ minor
(4 sharps = F, C, G, D)

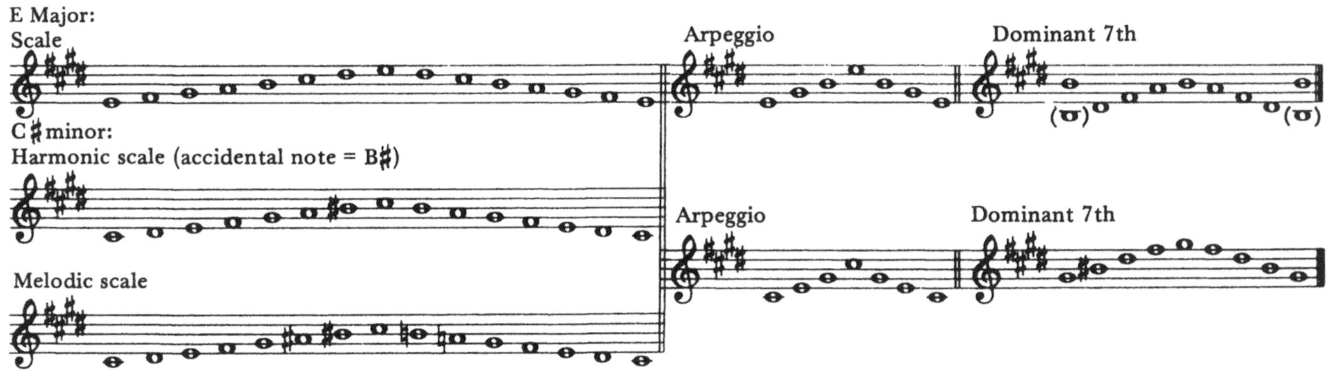

Piano

Louis Moyse Flute Collection

Louis Moyse

THE FLUTIST'S PRIMER

Easy and Melodious Exercises

Based on Scales and Arpeggios (in all Keys) with optional 2nd Flute or Piano Accompaniment

ED-3077

ISBN 0-7935-5005-X

G. SCHIRMER, Inc.

Distributed By
HAL•LEONARD® CORPORATION
7777 W. Bluemound Rd. P.O. Box 13819 Milwaukee, WI 53213

To Heather Allen-Moyse

The Flutist's Primer

Easy and Melodious Exercises
based on Scales and Arpeggios (in all keys)
with optional 2nd flute, or piano accompaniment

Louis Moyse

PART I

1
C Major - A minor

A minor

2
G Major - E minor
(1 sharp = F)

G Major

E minor

3
F Major - D minor
(1 flat = B)

F Major

D minor

4
D Major - B minor
(2 sharps = F, C)

B minor

5

B♭ Major - G minor

(2 flats = B, E)

B♭ Major

G minor

6
A Major - F♯ minor
(3 sharps = F, C, G)

F# minor

7
E♭ Major - C minor
(3 flats = B, E, A)

E♭ Major

C minor

8

E Major - C# minor

(4 sharps = F, C, G, D)

E Major

C♯ minor

9
A♭ Major - F minor
(4 flats = B, E, A, D)

A♭ Major

F minor

10
B Major - G♯ minor
(5 sharps = F, C, G, D, A)

G♯ minor

11
D♭ Major - B♭ minor
(5 Flats = B, E, A, D, G)

B♭ minor

12
F# Major - D# minor
(6 Sharps = F, C, G, D, A, E)

F# Major
(Mozart: Twinkle, Twinkle, Little Star tune)

D♯ minor
(The same tune in minor)
Fine
Fine
D. C. al Fine
(senza replica)
D. C. al Fine
(senza replica)

C♯ minor

9
A♭ Major - F minor
(4 flats = B, E, A, D)

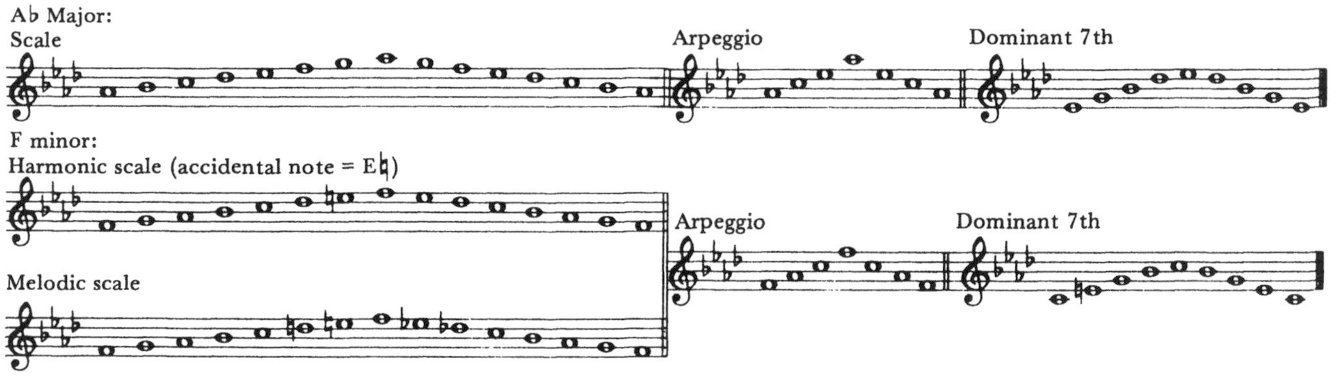

F minor

10
B Major - G♯ minor
(5 sharps = F, C, G, D, A)
(Enharmonic scales = C♭ Major - A♭ minor
7 flats = B, E, A, D, G, C, F)

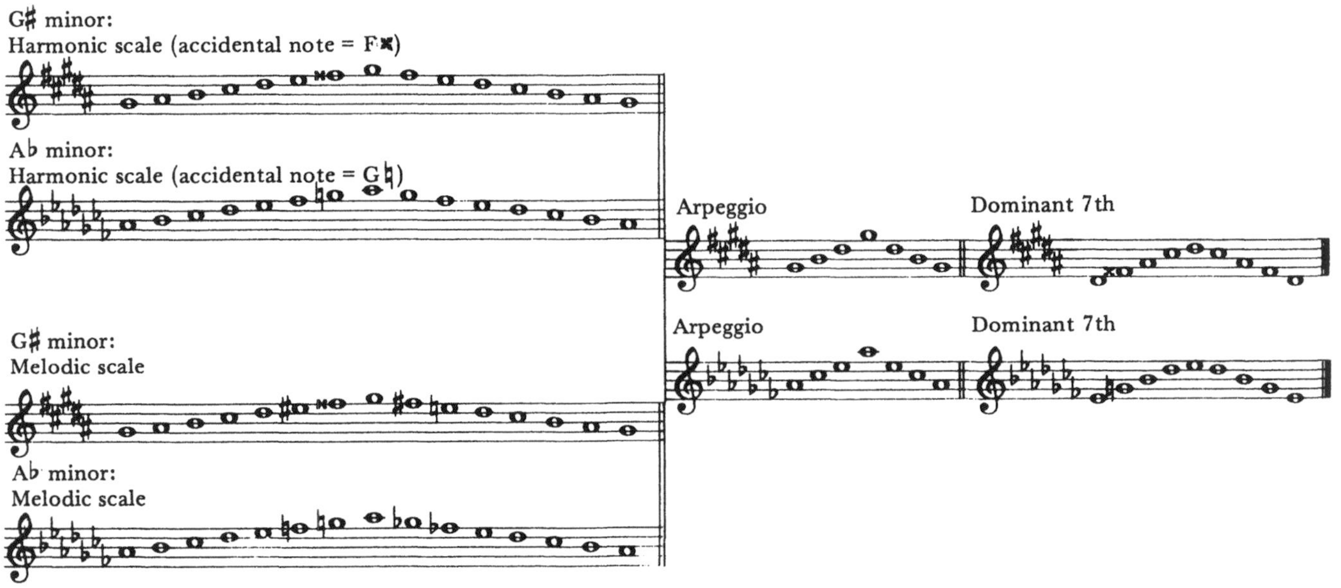

B Major

G♯ minor

11
D♭ Major - B♭ minor
(5 Flats = B, E, A, D, G)
(Enharmonic scales = C♯ Major - A♯ minor
7 sharps = F, C, G, D, A, E, B)

D♭ Major:
Scale | Arpeggio | Dominant 7th

C♯ Major:
Scale | Arpeggio | Dominant 7th

B♭ minor:
Harmonic scale (accidental note = A♮)

A♯ minor:
Harmonic scale (accidental note = G𝄪)

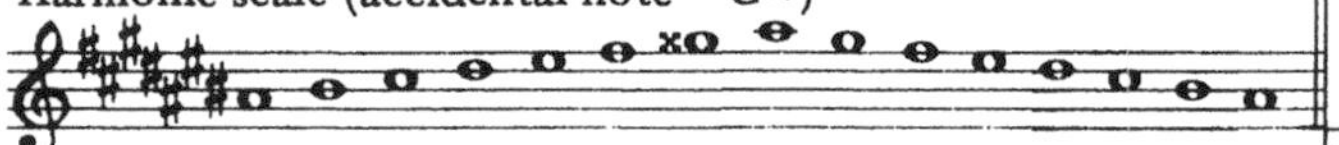

Arpeggio | Dominant 7th

Arpeggio | Dominant 7th

B♭ minor:
Melodic scale

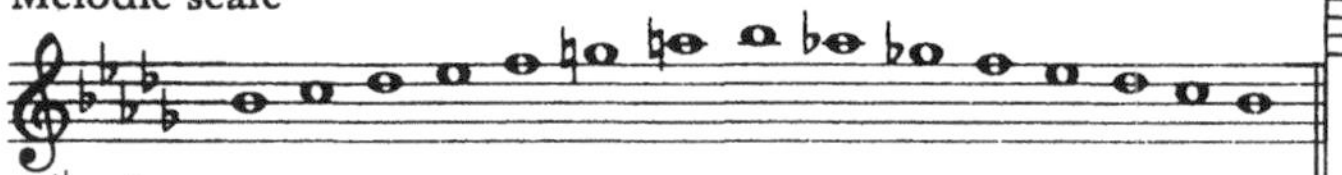

A♯ minor:
Melodic scale

D♭ Major

B♭ minor

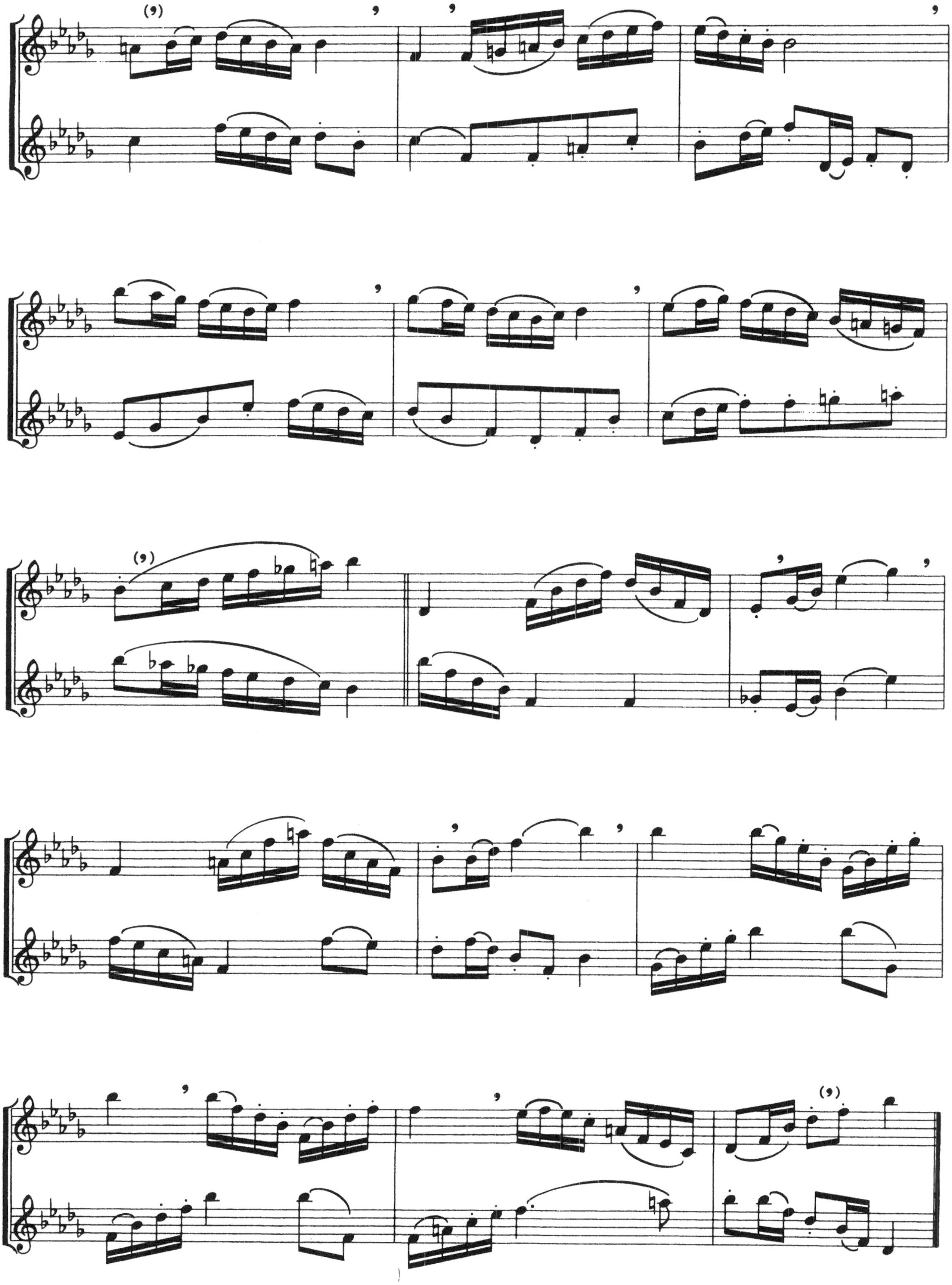

12
F♯ Major - D♯ minor
(6 Sharps = F, C, G, D, A, E)
(Enharmonic scales = G♭ Major - E♭ minor
6 flats = B, E, A, D, G, C)

F♯ Major:
Scale

Arpeggio

Dominant 7th

G♭ Major:
Scale

Arpeggio

Dominant 7th

D♯ minor:
Harmonic scale (accidental note = C𝄪)

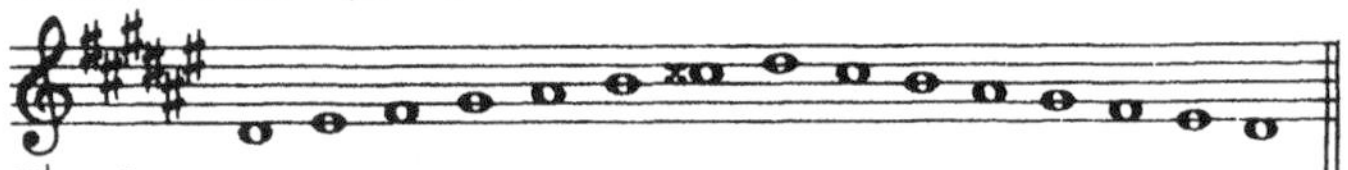

E♭ minor:
Harmonic scale (accidental note = D♮)

Arpeggio

Dominant 7th

Arpeggio

Dominant 7th

D♯ minor:
Melodic scale

E♭ minor:
Melodic scale

F♯ Major
(Mozart: Twinkle, Twinkle, Little Star tune)

D♯ minor
(The same tune in minor)

After playing the last number of scales and arpeggios, one can notice that the third register of the flute (high notes) has not yet been approached. This omission has been done on purpose, because the third octave of the flute is more difficult for both the lip pressure and fingerings. In order to complete and get the full benefit of this book, it is strongly recommended *(indeed it is a must)* that one start again at the beginning and practice all the exercises over again *one octave higher*. This only applies to the student; the second flute part, and piano accompaniment, should remain as they have been written.

When the student has concluded this book for a second time, it is hoped he or she is convinced of the utility and indispensability of practicing scales and arpeggios. Now, let us approach them on a purely technical basis.

PART II contains some easy exercises in elementary form. These will allow the student to master his technique on a higher level, and to achieve a better and deeper knowledge of his instrument.

PART II

Basic and Technical Exercises on Scales and Arpeggios (triads and 7th chords).

Practice these exercises by following the numbers as shown on the chart below.

Example: No. 1 - Major scale on C, page 29

No. 2 - Four triads (arpeggios) on C, page 30

No. 3 - Minor scale on A, page 32

No. 4 - Five 7th chords on A, page 34

No. 5 - Major scale on G, page 29, etc.

CHART

(Read from left to right)

Major scales on:	Four triads on:	Minor scales on:	Five 7th chords on:
No. 1 - C page 29	No. 2 - C page 30	No. 3 - A page 32	No. 4 - A page 34
No. 5 - G page 29	No. 6 - G page 31	No. 7 - E page 32	No. 8 - E page 33
No. 9 - F page 29	No. 10 - page 30-31	No. 11 - D page 32	No. 12 - D page 33
No. 13 - D page 29	No. 14 - D page 30	No. 15 - B page 32	No. 16 - B page 34
No. 17 - B♭ page 29	No. 18 - B♭ page 31	No. 19 - G page 32	No. 20 - G page 34
No. 21 - A page 29	No. 22 - A page 31	No. 23 - F♯ page 32	No. 24 - F♯ page 33
No. 25 - E♭ page 29	No. 26 - E♭ page 30	No. 27 - C page 32	No. 28 C page 32
No. 29 - E page 29	No. 30 - E page 30	No. 31 - C♯ page 32	No. 32 - C♯ page 32
No. 33 - A♭ page 29	No. 34 - A♭ page 31	No. 35 - F page 32	No. 36 - F page 33
No. 37 - B (or C♭) page 29	No. 38 - B page 31	No. 39 - G♯ (or A♭) page 32	No. 40 - A♭ (or G♯) page 34
No. 41 - D♭ (or C♯) page 29	No. 42 - C♯ (or D♭) page 30	No. 43 - B♭ (or A♯) page 32	No. 44 - B♭ (or A♯) page 34
No. 45 - F♯ (or G♭) page 29	No. 46 - F♯ (or G♭) page 30 - 31	No. 47 - D♯ (or E♭) page 32	No. 48 - E♭ (or D♯) page 33

For all the major and minor scales, the printed models (on page 29 and 32) must be used; add the number of sharps or flats which are involved in the key signature scale you are practicing.

For the triads (arpeggios) and 7th chords, different combinations of chords are printed in the section under the number given. Use the model in its entirety for each separate chord.

Major Scales

Legato (slur) - Repeat each section 4 times as in examples I, II and III according to the student's breathing capacity and the speed at which it is played. In all examples, observe carefully the second beat rest (note the arrows). This will give the student a better sense of the rhythm as well as allowing his mind and fingers to rest.

Example I

Example II

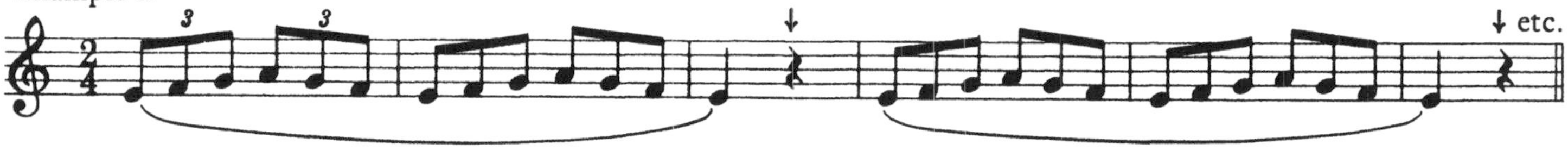

Example III

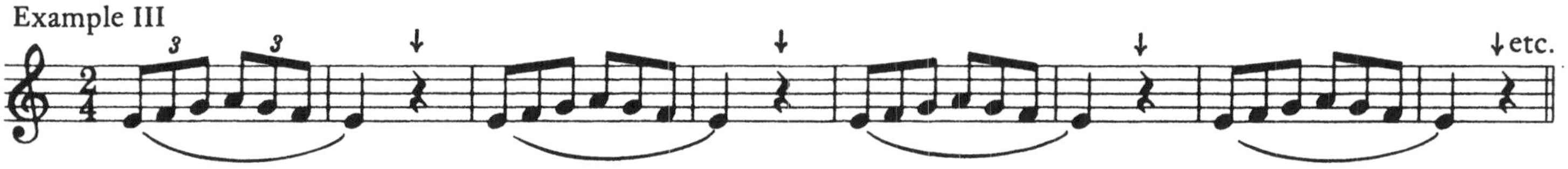

Triads (arpeggios)

* These chords require a low B Key on the flute = If you have it, start the model at the very beginning (first section)
If you do not have it, start the model from the 2nd section.

* These chords require a low B Key on the flute = If you have it, start the model at the very beginning (first section)
If you do not have it, start the model from the 2nd section.

Minor Scales

The accidental note between ( ) has to be played according to the rule about harmonic minor scales.

(Same as Major scales; repeat each section 4 times, legato.)

7th Chords

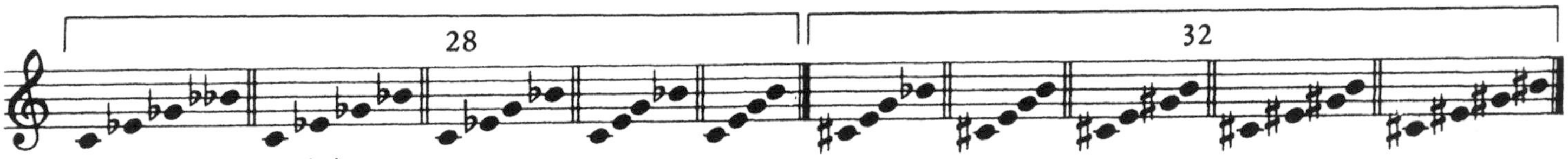

(same as scales; repeat 4 times each section, legato)

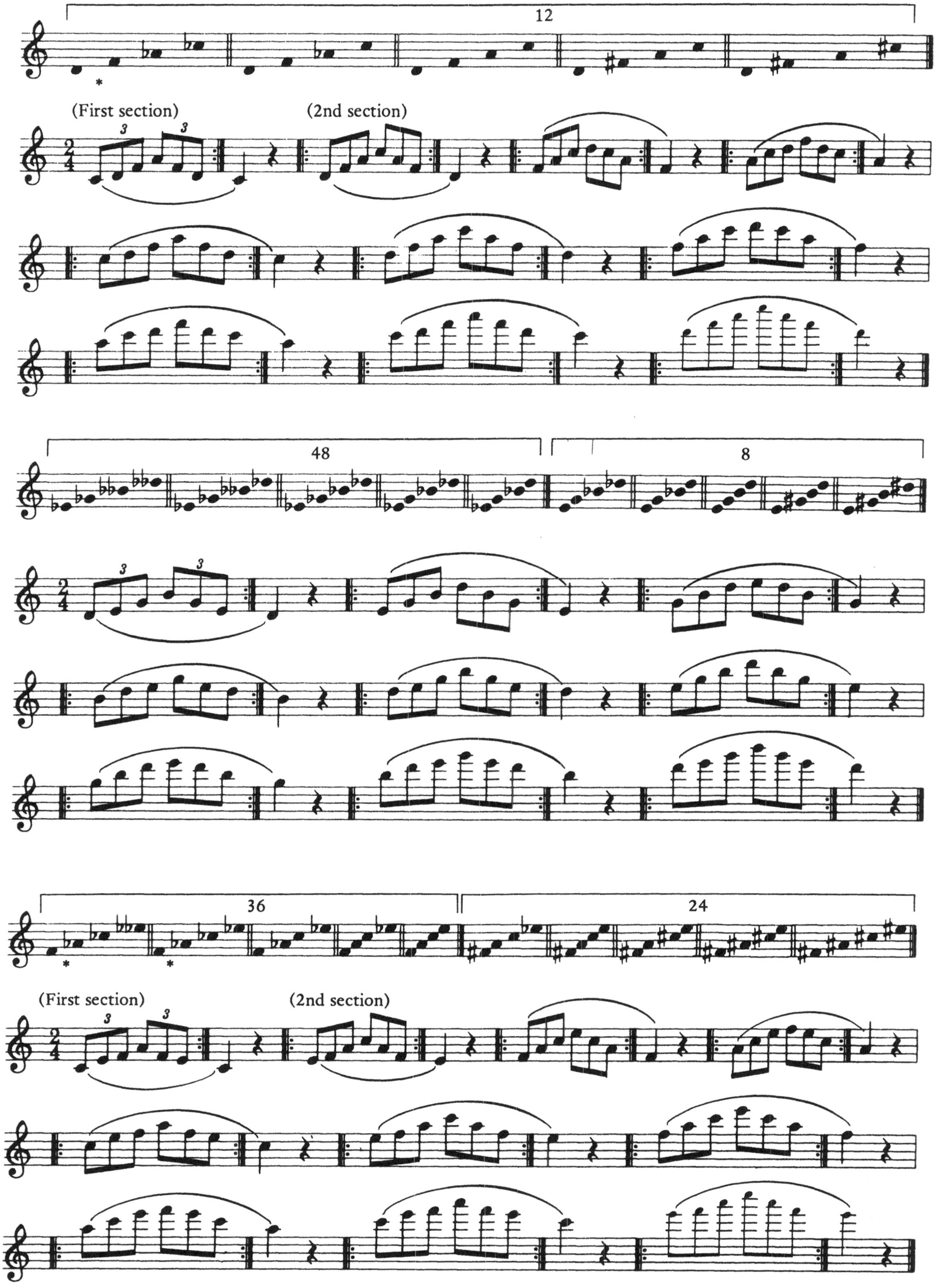

* See footnote on page 31.

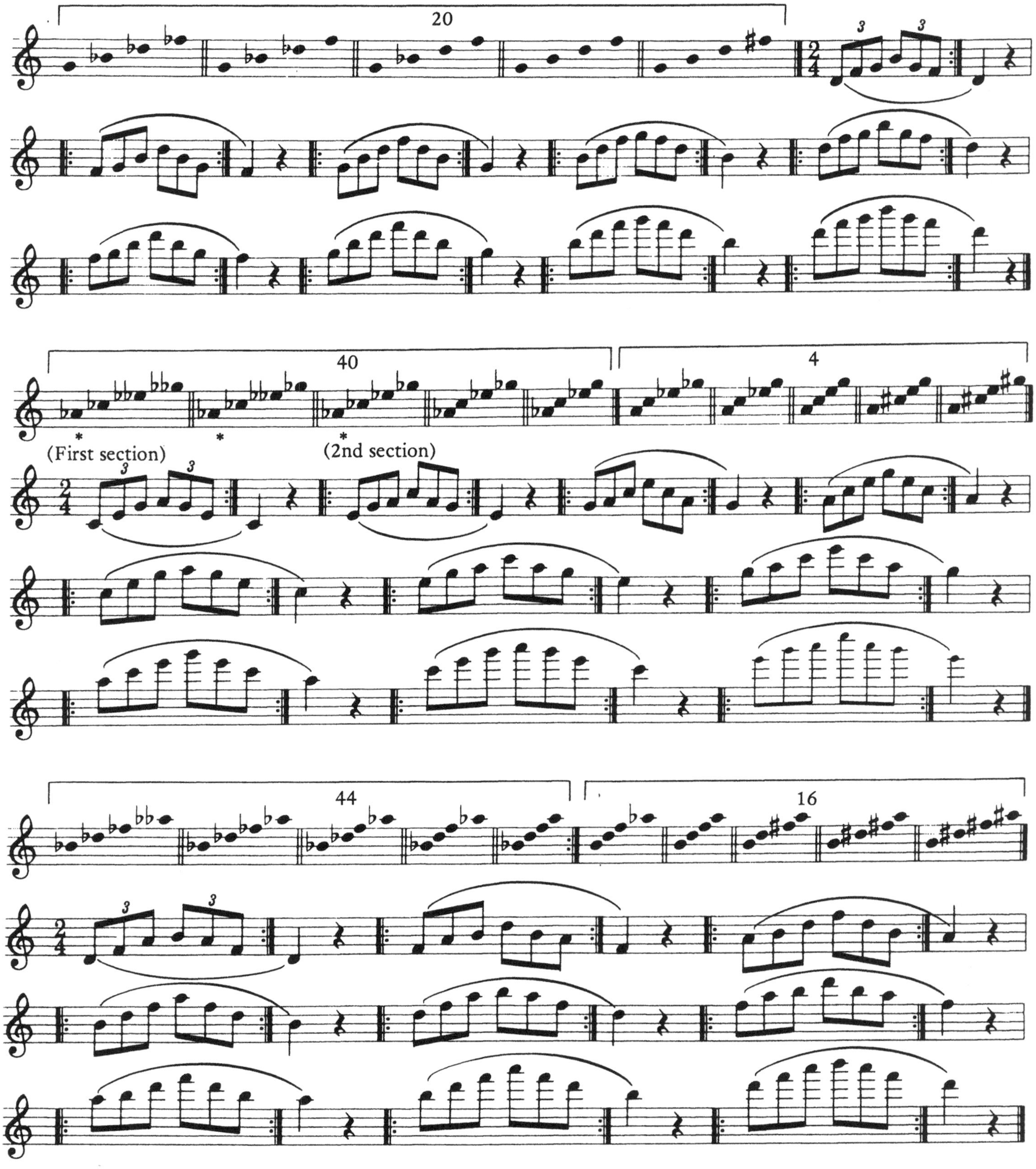

All these exercises can also be very profitable when practiced in a 4 ( ) rhythm instead of a 3 ( ) rhythm as written in Part II. The student should add the next note of the scale or chord to each section, as in the examples below:

Major and minor scales =

Triads (arpeggio) =

7th chords =

* See footnote on page 31.